Affirmations
For Men
365 Powerful & Positive Daily Affirmations to Reprogram your Mind.

Daniel Caldwell

©Copyright 2021 by Idyll Publishing
All rights reserved.
It is not legal to reproduce, duplicate, or transmit any part of this document in either electronic means or in printed format. Recording of this publication is strictly prohibited.

Prologue

In life, we all face adversity in different shapes and forms. And at some point your morale may take a hit. However, it is how we react to these hardships that define us. Understanding our ability to face these adversities is where magnificent wonders can occur.

Have you ever caught yourself contemplating self-sabotaging beliefs and thought why am I thinking like this?
This self-defeating rationale can drastically destroy your character and spiral you further down into deeper depths of destruction.

Learning to cultivate more appreciation and gratefulness can take time. However, with practice, you can retrain and strengthen your perspective. This is where affirmations come into play. The mind is a powerful force, and reprogramming your thinking can have lasting positive effects on your overall health and well-being.

What are affirmations you may ask? Positive affirmations are statements to help replace negative judgments with powerful and positive thoughts. They remind you of how far you've come, what you value most, and what you're capable of accomplishing.

These powerful affirmations are a great starting point to help encourage motivation and reclaim your true potential. You can read one a day, or all of them. The more you read and affirm in these ideas the more likely you will start to believe in them.

Personally, I find the best time to practice my affirmations is first thing in the morning straight after jumping out of bed. I repeat my favorite affirmations several times out loud before going about my day.

If you resonate with a select few of these affirmations, add them to your own personal routine and slowly add more overtime. Know that it's easy to create your own affirmations too. Bend and mold any of these statements to other areas of your life you want to improve, but keep them positive. Let's get into it!

1.
I am not here for nothing. I am here for everything.

2.
Today, I am going to push myself harder. I will only stop when I feel confident I have given my best.

3.
I am grateful for the man I am becoming.

4.
Fear is only a feeling. It will not hold me back.

5.
All of my problems have a solution.

6.
It's not what happens, but how I react that matters.

7.
I will not be stopped today.

8.
I am aware of my priorities and I will focus on them before all else.

9.
With the new day comes new strength and new thoughts.

10.
To be calm is the highest achievement of the self.

11.
I matter. My beliefs matter. My voice matters.

12.
I am equipped to go that extra mile.

13.
Life begins at the end of my comfort zone.

14.
I believe that I hold the strength within to achieve all of my dreams.

15.
I choose to challenge myself to reach greater heights.

16.
I am letting go of all that no longer serves me.

17.
I am centered, calm, and sharp.

18.
I expect nothing but appreciate everything.

19.
The obstacle is often the way.

20.
The time for change is now.

21.
I will seize every opportunity presented before me.

22.
I am limited only by my vision of what is possible.

23.
I can view any situation from multiple perspectives.

24.
What's next is next. I have to take care of what is in front of me first.

25.
My level of success centers around my effort.

26.
What a privilege it is to be alive, to think, to enjoy, to love.

27.
Every life experience presents an opportunity to become wiser.

28.
My passion is ready to reveal itself.

29.
I can and I will.

30.
I need nothing more, as I am content with less.

31.
My mind and heart are clear.

32.
Nothing can stop me.

33.
I wake up each day inspired.

34.
I will set clear goals and work to complete them every day.

35.
I will be stronger than my strongest excuse.

36.
Fall seven times, stand up eight.

37.
I am a warrior, a fighter, and I will always persevere.

38.
I am an enormous inspiration to those around me.

39.
I am a man of substance. I am intrigued by everything.

40.
I am successful.

41.
My capacity to conquer is limitless.

42.
My mind is focused and ready to commit.

43.
I maintain strength, clarity, and peace of mind.

44.
When I declutter my life, my focus gets sharper and sharper.

45.
I boldly approach every challenge strategically.

46.
I value my time and input.

47.
My mind is full of brilliant and innovative ideas.

48.
I can do anything I set my mind to if I am willing to pay the price for greatness.

49.
I have the power to change my story.

50.
My strong work ethic is unquestionable.

51.

I am disciplined.

52.

I am forever evolving.

53.

I find inspiration in the world around me.

54.

With hard work and effort, I will succeed.

55.

I have unlimited potential.

56.
Money flows freely to me.

57.
I use obstacles to motivate me to learn and grow.

58.
I grow wiser with each passing day.

59.
I will stand up for what I believe in.

60.
I can handle anything life throws me.

61.

By exercising, I become an amazing role model for others.

62.

I am content with less.

63.

I will not let regret hold me back.

64.

I am at peace with all that has happened.

65.

I am worthy of all the compassion and kindness life has to offer.

66.
I am dedicated to building a stronger body.

67.
My success is based off of my willingness to work hard no matter what obstacles stand in my way.

68.
I see failures as a chance to learn.

69.
I understand the beginnings of all things are small, and I will persevere until I find success.

70.
I am a leader.

71.
I am capable of any feat.

72.
I deserve to be healthy and strong.

73.
I am on the right track and my future looks promising.

74.
I can take lead in any social situation if required.

75.
I will commit to getting a better sleep every night.

76.
If I am no longer able to change a situation, I will challenge to change myself.

77.
I will treat myself gently when I am going through tough times and need a break.

78.
I am willing to do what it takes to become successful.

79.
Whatever happens at all happens as it should.

80.
I attract fortune and wealth.

81.
My confidence knows no limit.

82.
Some of the best opportunities will be made, not found.

83.
I am an asset to anything I am involved in.

84.
My strength is greater than any struggle.

85.
My driving force comes from within.

86.
I will nourish my body with healthy and nutritious foods, and my body will be thankful.

87.
Everything that is happening now is happening for ultimate good.

88.
My world changes with my mindset and thoughts.

89.
I will encourage those around me to do great things.

90.
I trust in the process.

91.
Each decision I make generates new opportunities.

92.
I am absolutely secure in who I am.

93.
I am not concerned in how others view me.

94.
I am excited for what the future holds for me.

95.
If it doesn't challenge me, it won't change me.

96.
I am grateful for everything that I receive.

97.
Broken bridges will not hinder my momentum.

98.
I deserve to feel healthy and lively.

99.
I choose to be happy.

100.
The only thing I can control is how I respond.

101.
I see the bigger picture.

102.
Others look up to me for my strength of character.

103.
Discipline is choosing between what I want now and what I want most.

104.
I treat myself with respect and kindness from today forward.

105.
My mental health is just as vital as my physical health.

106.
I hold the power to create the success and build the wealth I desire.

107.
I am dedicated to self-improvement.

108.
I remain focused at the task at hand.

109.
It is okay to be vulnerable.

110.
The world craves my exclusivity.

111.
I wake up each morning with intent and purpose.

112.
I am confident in my ability to do great things.

113.
I radiate joy and enthusiasm.

114.
I will always speak my mind.

115.
Anything or anyone that angers me will not control my mood.

116.
I will never give anyone the right to rescind my pride.

117.
Even the darkest night will end and the sun will rise.

118.
I am innovative and tenacious.

119.
I gain pleasure from helping others.

120.
I will not give up in times of hardship.

121.

I'm proud of who I becoming.

122.

I value my worth.

123.

I am supported, safe, and free.

124.

I am open to abundance, joy, and pleasure.

125.

I feel empowered to ask for help when I need it.

126.
Where others see a trial, I see new prospects.

127.
I no longer fake my character to impress people.

128.
I will remain true to my word.

129.
I am a great listener and open to help others in times of need.

130.
I will compare myself to who I was yesterday, not to who someone else is today.

131.
No-one is better at being me than me.

132.
I am thankful for my strength, my health, and my vitality.

133.
I am building the foundations of a magnificent future.

134.
I won't let someone else's opinion of me shape my reality.

135.
My will is iron clad.

136.
Failure builds character.

137.
I am a powerhouse. I am indestructible.

138.
My mind is sharp and ready to take on whatever awaits.

139.
I continuously strive to improve my processes.

140.
I realize that the best view comes after the hardest climb.

141.
I am doing the best I can.

142.
My inner strength and resilience increase every day.

143.
I promise to myself that I will exercise more healthy habits.

144.
A river of compassion washes away my anger and replaces it with love.

145.
The best preparation for tomorrow is doing my best today.

146.
I am charismatic and magnetic.

147.
I will not retreat from discomfort. I will embrace it, and I will grow from it.

148.
I release every block that held me back from receiving prosperity.

149.
I trust myself to make the correct decision.

150.
I give myself permission to prosper and grow.

151.
I see the best in everyone.

152.
I greet every new challenge with enthusiasm.

153.
Happiness is a choice; today, I choose to be happy.

154.
My emotions are just as important as anyone else's.

155.
I will waste no more time arguing what a good man should be. I will be one.

156.
I deserve to give and receive love.

157.
It's my road and mine alone. Others may walk with it with me, but no one can walk it for me.

158.
I am ready to achieve greatness.

159.
I do what needs to be done, whether I feel like or not.

160.
Calm is my primary state of being.

161.
I am safe and sound. All is well.

162.
My strong work ethic helps me to achieve my goals.

163.
I stand with brilliant posture and vigor.

164.
I no longer allow myself to be distracted from my goals.

165.
I appreciate all that I have.

166.
I can clearly and confidently express my emotions.

167.
I narrate the story of my life.

168.
I release all stress and criticisms towards myself and forgive.

169.
I am becoming the very best version of myself.

170.
I am determined to be healthier day by day.

171.
I am ready to explore my passion.

172.
I allow myself to express my thoughts in an organized manner.

173.
I choose to let go of overthinking, and will just do what needs to be done.

174.
I realize my priorities and I am clear about what is more important in life.

175.
I invest my time and energy wisely, towards more meaningful things.

176.
My opinions and ideas are respected and valued.

177.
I always see the positive in every situation.

178.
I am an unstoppable force of nature.

179.
I am done with delaying what needs to be done. I will take action.

180.
I approach myself with patience and understanding.

181.
I am capable of healing.

182.
I rise up to any challenge that comes my way.

183.
Small changes on a daily basis lead to massive changes over time.

184.
I am grateful for my existence.

185.
I know when to trust my intuition.

186.

Confusion is a temporary state. Eventually, the mind will reorganize itself and regain clarity. All I need to do is be patient.

187.

Every morning I wake up with a desire to triumph.

188.

My body is healthy and full of energy.

189.

I am a living, breathing example of motivation.

190.

I align my goals with the higher purpose of my life.

191.
I see the beauty in everything.

192.
I don't sweat the small stuff. It's not worth it.

193.
I will face today with unwavering confidence.

194.
My drive and ambition allow me to achieve my goals.

195.
I am intelligent and focused.

196.
One day at a time.

197.
I can remain calm, even in moments of chaos.

198.
Working out helps to clear my mind.

199.
I am getting better and better with every passing day.

200.
I have made mistakes, but I will not let them define me.

201.

Creative energy flows through me and leads me to brilliant new ideas.

202.

I finish what matters and let go of what does not.

203.

I know what I value and what I don't.

204.

I set myself free and forgive myself of any wrongdoings.

205.

I focus on what is in my power, and ignore what I can't control.

206.
My potential to succeed is infinite.

207.
I have everything I need to succeed.

208.
My actions make a big difference.

209.
I can retrieve any information from my subconscious mind by simply asking for it in a calm and relaxed manner.

210.
I have a grateful heart and a happy mind.

211.

The key to unleash my confidence is to do things on time and beat procrastination.

212.

In every situation, life is asking me a question, and my actions are my answer.

213.

I am independent and self-sufficient.

214.

I am extraordinarily adventurous.

215.

What I have done today was the best I was able to do today. And for that, I am thankful.

216.
I can and I will. End of story.

217.
I begin to gain clarity as I put my intention towards it.

218.
Stepping outside of my comfort zone is crucial for growth.

219.
I am a proactive problem-solver.

220.
I am my own superhero.

221.
I choose to stop apologizing for being myself.

222.
I will follow my heart's desire and ignore the masses.

223.
I take charge of my life.

224.
I am focused on the present and enjoying my time right now.

225.
I'm allowed to lean on others when I feel out of my depth.

226.
I wake up full of energy.

227.
I possess the humility required to ask questions and keep learning.

228.
I can accept criticism without taking offence.

229.
I am fueled by passion for what I do.

230.
I am courageous and ready to face my fears.

231.
I am hardworking and determined.

232.
I inhale confidence, and exhale fear.

233.
I will stay true to my word.

234.
I am learning to support myself to the best of my ability.

235.
If I fall, I get back up.

236.
I am far more effective when I take a moment for self-care.

237.
It's okay to not feel great today. Tomorrow is a new day.

238.
I am worthy of what I desire.

239.
I am aligned with my purpose.

240.
The journey of a thousand miles begins with one step.

241.
I have a much better memory than I give credit for.

242.
I am almost at the finish line.

243.
Every day I discover new and exciting paths to pursue.

244.
I feel incredible when I have accomplished a goal.

245.
There is no gain without struggle.

246.
I can transform obstacles into opportunities to better myself.

247.
I am an example of integrity, even when no one is watching.

248.
My overall health and mood have improved as a result of my exercise.

249.
Progress and effort is all that matters.

250.
I have an unshakable perseverance.

251.

I allow my mind to take a moment to analyze and regain clarity.

252.

Today, I will make 3 others smile.

253.

My well-being is my top priority.

254.

I will never have to do today again.

255.

My anxiety is motivation to adapt and improve.

256.
I can endure.

257.
I am always prepared. Hence, luck seems to favor me.

258.
My attitude permeates all external conditions

259.
I wish happiness and success for everyone.

260.
I will invest in myself.

261.
Every experience is a lesson. Every loss is a gain.

262.
My worth is not defined by my to-do list.

263.
I accept the things I cannot change.

264.
I am committed to making productive changes.

265.
I will give myself time to rest and heal. Tomorrow I will come back stronger.

266.
Success is in my blood.

267.
I realize that success is a result of precise thinking and hard work. I excel in both.

268.
I refuse to settle for less when I know I have more in me.

269.
Hardships are simply shortcuts to something better than I had planned.

270.
I am ever expanding my belief of what is possible.

271.
My daily goals will ensure that I reach my long term goals.

272.
Day by day. Thought by thought. I am progressing toward a better life.

273.
Not everything that weighs me down is mine to carry.

274.
I thrive in any opportunity that enables me to grow.

275.
Today I release old habits and uncover new pathways.

276.
I am proud of myself for trying.

277.
Each and every day I reach deeper levels of self-realization.

278.
The apex of every success is another step towards my growth.

279.
I am always in the right place at the right time.

280.
I am open and ready to receive miracles.

281.
My consciousness always expands to embrace new opportunities in my life.

282.
I will focus on today, one hour at a time.

283.
I know that each step forward launches me towards my end goal.

284.
I give myself time to learn and grow.

285.
I am getting to know myself on a deeper level.

286.
Each and every day I learn new lessons, expand my awareness, and develop my abilities.

287.
I am daring to be different.

288.
I am open and receptive to new avenues of income.

289.
I will celebrate each milestone on my pathway to success.

290.
No more letting bad days distract me from my goals.

291.
Self-care is not selfish.

292.
I dare to detest mediocrity, and be great

293.
Everything is going to work out fine.

294.
Even as I stretch and strive to be who I can be, I am happy with who I am now.

295.
I am going to give my best until my goals are complete.

296.
I am not alone in my struggles.

297.
My opportunities multiply as they are seized.

298.
What matters is who I am, not who I have been.

299.
Good things are unfolding in front of me.

300.
I will commit to building a future that serves me.

301.
By failing to prepare, I am preparing to fail.

302.
Today, I choose success.

303.
I understand that I do not know everything. But, I am willing to learn.

304.
I surround myself with positive people who will help bring out the best in me.

305.
I am courageous enough to at least try new things.

306.

I accept myself unconditionally.

307.

All is well.

308.

My past is not a reflection of my future.

309.

I am strong. I am energized. I am motivated.

310.

I am in complete control in how I react to others.

311.

If I want something new, I have to adapt new habits.

312.

Difficult times allow me to appreciate the good times.

313.

No amount of stress and worry can change the future.

314.

I gratefully receive the lessons that each experience brings.

315.

My mind is energized, clear and focused.

316.

My friends and family enrich my life beyond measure.

317.

No one is better at my job than I am.

318.

My actions create constant prosperity.

319.

I am comfortable knowing that I have the resources and knowledge to support myself.

320.

I recognize every blessing, no matter how small.

321.
All that separates me from my goals is my effort.

322.
I honor my body by trusting the signals it sends me.

323.
I am healthy. I am wise. I am wealthy.

324.
I understand that the difference between success and failure is my ability to take action.

325.
I am grateful for the challenges I have survived in my life.

326.
This stressful experience does not control me.

327.
My presence is my power.

328.
I am deeply fulfilled by what I do.

329.
I am choosing and not waiting to be chosen.

330.
I am always eager to learn and develop.

331.
I am not afraid of living authentically.

332.
I am willing to explore uncharted territory.

333.
Today, I will take a big step forward towards my goals.

334.
I'm choosing the rest of my life the best of my life.

335.
I refuse to give up as I have not trialed every option.

336.
In order to build self-discipline, I have to work on myself even when I don't feel like it.

337.
I am present in the moment.

338.
I am a genuine caring person.

339.
I will live my life as the exciting adventure that it is.

340.
My intelligence allows me the ability to adapt to change.

341.
I can be scared and still perform.

342.
I am living in total abundance.

343.
I radiate positive energy.

344.
I am thankful for my unique creativity.

345.
If I am to fail, I will turn it into an opportunity to begin again, only more intelligently.

346.
I manifest perfect health by making smart decisions.

347.
My wins are coming soon. I just have to remain patient and keep working.

348.
I will take action and get things done.

349.
Today I decide to live with hope and optimism.

350.
I believe in my ability.

351.

I see failures as stepping stones.

352.

I see abundance all around me.

353.

Today is my chance to excel.

354.

I am calm and at ease.

355.

I will turn my dreams into goals. Goals into steps. Steps into actions. And I will accomplish one action per day.

356.
I am the CEO of my life.

357.
I will face difficult situations with grace and courage.

358.
My work has purpose and transforms people's lives.

359.
I embrace this path that I am on right now.

360.
I am blessed, and highly favoured.

361.
I am fearless and courageous.

362.
To take care of others, I must first take care of myself.

363.
Every person I meet can teach me something. I am grateful for their wisdom.

364.
I am poised to attract success and happiness.

365.
My work has purpose and transforms people's lives.

Epilogue

This year has been tough. We've all suffered through tremendous hardships and setbacks. You deserve a huge pat on the back for making it this far. Great work and keep pushing forward!

Remember, these positive affirmations can be implemented into your daily routine, whether it be right before you jump into bed, or just before work in the morning. The important part is that you are taking care of yourself.

Some days will always be harder than others, but understand that you are amazing and can conquer anything set in front of you!

Keep affirming your greatness. You got this!

If you liked this book, it would be sincerely appreciated if you could leave a review on Amazon. Let me know what you liked or even what you didn't like, as it helps me release better books in the future.
-Daniel Caldwell

www.ingramcontent.com/pod-product-compliance
Lightning Source LLC
Chambersburg PA
CBHW071754080526
44588CB00013B/2232